SONNETS
FOR DARK TIMES

Life in fourteen lines, or four years '
measured out fourteen lines at a time.
Four years to remember, although often
all we wanted was to forget them.
Writing these sonnets helped
make dark times less dark, helped
put frustrations and worries aside
long enough to celebrate and share
the magic of living with the right person
surrounded by beauty under so many
mysterious and beautiful mountains....

SONNETS

FOR DARK TIMES

2017–2020

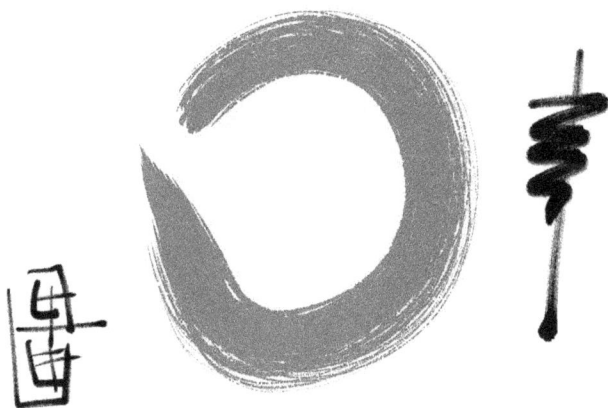

LITO**TEJADA**FLORES

WESTERN EYE PRESS

2021

Sonnets for Dark Times
is published by Western Eye Press,
a small independent press
(very small and very independent)
with a home base under
the Sangre de Cristo mountains
in the Colorado Rockies

© 2021 Lito Tejada-Flores
Western Eye Press
PO Box 2, Crestone CO 81131

www.WesternEyePress.com
ISBN13: 978-0-941283-53-3 paperback
ISBN13: 978-0-941283-55-7 eBook
Book design, the cover photo,
of Lago Chelenko, Patagonia,
and digital brushwork by the author.
The type is Optima by Herman Zapf,
a 20th-Century classic

CONTENTS

2 0 1 7
NEW SONNETS

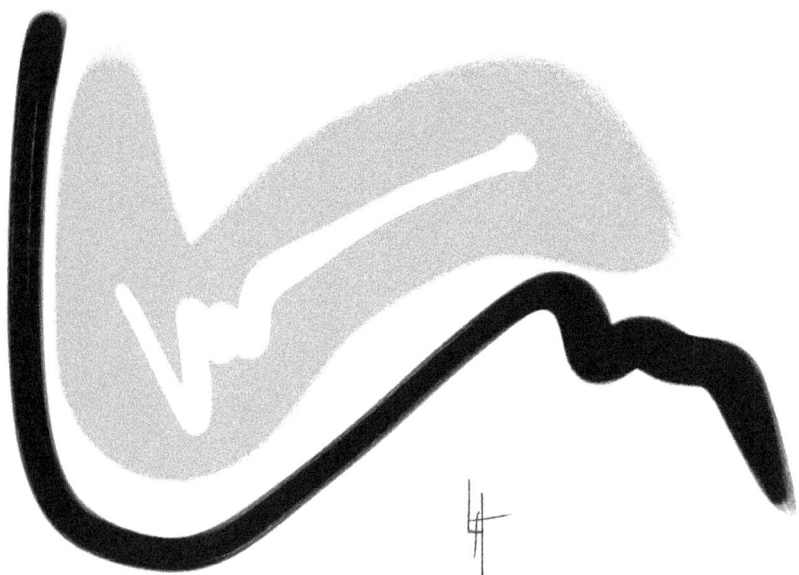

UNITED STATES OF YESTERDAY

Lemmings headed for the cliff, following this pied piper
Backward, toward yesterday, the happy mob, laughing, joking,
How long before they wake up? Not long or maybe never.
And what a painful awakening, waiting for us, all of us.

How many warnings, how many times, how many chances
Do we get? Is this it? Is it over? That's what it feels like.
Is there another act? Or is this act three? No curtain call.
Everything ends, sure, but right now?... We aren't ready.

Never will be. And why not? Why didn't we see it coming?
Have to do better. Can we? Is it already too late?
Too many desperate daily questions with no answers.

OK, we won't, we can't wait for answers, let's go. . . .
Even if we don't know the answer, we can still be part of it,
Turn our backs on greedhead capitalism, start over.

(UN)CIVIL WAR

It's almost a civil war, an uncivil war,
Some things never change, still trying
To keep black people from voting,
Women from working, not to pay taxes. . . .

A fight to the death—of democracy,
A lesson in savage indifference,
Refusing to help—anyone, any time,
Me-first madness, a cult of selfishness.

The Republican wrecking crew in charge
But flailing, a moment's opportunity
To resist, restart, rebuild the world.

A civil war with no leader, no Lincoln.
Lots of passion, less compassion,
A just cause, just out of reach, or. . .

SLOWLY

Watching the sky turn slowly pink
The blue shadow of the earth sink
Slowly behind the peaks, the lake
Gather the first light, give it back.

Slowly watching the world turn,
Yesterday sliding out of sight
Behind our backs, today pausing
To select its new colors, new clouds. . .

The world wakes up as slowly as we do.
We rub our eyes, rub away last night,
Its laughter, wine, troubled dreams.

The world waits for antarctic winds,
Southern storms, volcanos, quakes,
To rub away this mess we've made.

THESE DAYS

What if? what if it only gets worse?
What if the good guys can't ever
Win again, down for the count?
Can't be, could but it isn't, or is it?

Tough times: a French filmmaker tells us
His kids asked him: Papa, if Le Pen wins
The election where can we live? The same
Doubts, same fears, in every country. . . .

Orcs on the march, the Shire is burning—
It isn't Middle Earth, it's the whole earth,
And it's for real. No one is strong enough

To solve this one by themselves,
Defeat the bad guys, put things right.
Maybe there are enough Hobbits to do it. .

EL FIN DEL MUNDO

We are a hemisphere away from that mean spirited government,
It's not far enough. Beyond the horizon, clouds are hiding
Not just Patagonian clouds, stacked lenticulars, wind torn,
But blacker and bleaker. We feel them a world away, and worry.

Tonight the lake is glassy smooth, reflecting a peaceful sky
Two raptors, *caracaras*, stand on the edge of the cliff for hours,
Patient? Bored? Waiting? Real Patagonians—"If you're in a hurry,
You lose time." Every one says so—here at the end of the world.

Looking west, waiting for sunset colors to paint this blue evening.
Looking north, as though we could see what's coming. We can't.
We don't really want to, because we know it won't be good.

The faintest pink, almost a sunset, up north almost a democracy,
We should keep our thoughts right here: this lake, these birds,
This evening, this life. Why look farther, north, beyond this horizon?

SAN LUIS VALLEY SPRINGTIME

Countdown to tomorrow—can't wait, but I will.
What's up? what's coming? what's next? what now?
So much we don't want, so much to dread.
But tomorrow the sun will climb into the sky

Again—again and again—almost forever . . .
Tonight is different, tonight nothing is certain,
And nothing is forever except this fight
Between good & bad—no, say it: good & evil.

Where does this spite come from?
This meanness, this callous greed?
No more health care, no help, no breaks . . .

But tax breaks for those who don't need them,
Fat cats getting fatter. . . Will tomorrow's sun
Be enough to keep going, keep fighting?

100 DAYS

How much damage can they do, could anyone do?
In 100 days? More than we could have guessed.
How long is it going to take to undo this disaster?
Not just 100 days. Will it even, ever, be possible?

Will there be anything left? We don't seem to care,
Too busy pretending it doesn't matter. It does.
Too busy doing everything we would have done
If life still made sense. Cooking dinner, planning trips.

We always said: everything changes. But no, not this fast.
Not forever. We cling to those cyclical myths—
History repeats itself. Does it? Something does.

Maybe just human folly, stubborn meanness,
A dark picture, the same lessons—never learned.
Only somehow we know this time it's different.

WAITING

Waiting for weather, is it worth the wait?
Waiting for a sign, a hint that all's not lost,
Waiting to see if so many bad yesterdays
Can add up to even one good tomorrow.

How long have we been waiting?
How long can the world wait, for us?
For us to wake up, or grow up, or
Shape up? It's been a long long wait.

And it isn't over. But it's time. Time
To say: no more, time to fight back,
Fight for those who can't: lost species,

Lakes, polar ice, penguins, people too.
We're next. It's not about saving the planet,
Just one last attempt to save ourselves.

WHY NOT

Why me? Why not?
Why you? Why not?
Not likely, but it's not over—
Not what we expected.

No choice anymore.
Is resistance real?
Can it work? Why not?
Is it working? Don't know.

We need a time out,
Need to start over,
Just one more chance.

This time we promise
We'll vote, this time
We promise to do it right.

TRUMP YEARS, TRUMP TEARS

IT'S A CAPITALIST COUP D'ÉTAT
MORE FAT FOR THE FAT CATS
LESS WORK FOR WORKERS
LESS HELP FOR THE HELPLESS

THIS TRUMP ADMINISTRATION
AN "UNPRESIDENTED" DISASTER
AN OLD FASHIONED KLEPTOCRACY
COMEBACK OF THE CRIMINAL CLASS

HOW MUCH CAN THEY STEAL?
AND HOW FAST? A WRECKING CREW
TRYING TO TURN BACK THE CLOCK

TOO LATE TO SAY NO THANKS
IT'S BROKEN AND WE BOUGHT IT
PLANETS DON'T SPIN BACKWARD

TODAY

Somewhere else, some other time, not now,
Not yet at any rate. . . and why not? why wait?
Why wait for tomorrow? Tomorrow's waiting for us,
To wake up, wake up & seize the day, *carpe diem*. . .

We just aren't ready—to own our lives, our future.
It can't happen here, can it? No more food, no jobs,
No electricity, no more stuff. . . Maybe, maybe not. . .
We don't know, worse yet, we don't really care.

Don't worry, you're not alone, nobody wants to change,
The problems are too big, the solutions too hard,
You can't save the planet, the region, even your town.

So what the hell can you do? should you do? Or not?
Wake up, greet the day, go for a long walk, watch clouds
Tangled in the sky, today tangled in forever. Here soon enough.

SO MANY QUESTIONS

It's who I am—no one else—but is it enough?
It's the life I live, my bet on the future,
Does it make sense? What are the odds?
Whose side am I on? Today? And tomorrow?

History's closing in on us, on everyone. . . .
This immense investment in yesterday—
How much can they roll back? And how fast?
Who'll be there to pick up the pieces?

The avalanche of now—will it bury us?
Are we strong enough to dig out the victims?
Where do we put them? Not them, they're us.

If we don't fight back we're all victims—
Austerity, inequality, brutality, the daily drumbeat,
How long do we have? Don't ask, just act!

PAIRS

It's now, it's never
It's today, it's tomorrow
It's life, it's death
It's joy, it's sorrow

It's time, it's too late
It's why, it's why not
It's right, it's wrong
It's too cold, too hot

It's a girl, it's a boy
It's false, it's true
It's night, it's day
It's too many, too few

It is what it is, not why
All we can do is try. . . .

CRESTONE SUMMER

9:15, still light outside, high summer's
Here with clouds of no-seeums.
We forgive them, take mesh bug shirts
On our morning hikes, grin and bear it.

The light's a bonus: five-alarm sunrises,
Sunsets worth waiting for, and by noon
The mosquitos have retreated out of sight.
We remember the south of France. . . .

White wine helps—can't find côtes de Provence
But it doesn't matter. What does? The shade
Of a canvas umbrella on a stone table? . . .

Should be enough. Enough that we're still here,
So many friends aren't. White cumulus clouds
Still rising over peaks, still there to admire.

COUNT TO 100

100 sonnets, 100 days to turn back the clock 100 years
100 reasons to be happy, or despair—is there a choice?
100 ways to say I love you, 100 more after that,
And then? Start over of course. Not just looking

For what's next, but imagining it, making it happen.
Sounds easy, it isn't. 100 ways to finish this story,
100 solutions to any equation, none quite right.
Nothing rhymes, nothing has to, but it has to work.

For some it never does, not their fault, no one's fault.
100 false solutions to real problems. 100 problems
We could solve if we really tried. Why don't we?

100 chances to get it right. We'll know when we do.
Why 100? It's only a number—every moment counts,
Every day, every decision, every sunrise, every kiss.

END OF THE SEASON

Summer racing toward the finish line
Sunflowers hanging on, but shriveling
Afternoon thunderstorms seal the deal
Somewhere behind the range, thunder.

And now the shadow of another season
Stretches out across the valley. Snakeweed
Announces a brighter autumn palette,
Change is everywhere, we have no choice.

Wake up ready for frost, it still isn't here
But will be soon. A big yellow school bus
Knits dirt roads into a daily two-hour route.

We are tired out from too much sunshine,
Too much bad news we can't fix, numb,
Waiting for winter's cold to wake us up.

EAST BAY

Berkeley 40 years on
Everything's the same
Everything is different
Freeways frozen full-time

Chez Panisse still here
But the Med is gone
Homeless encampments
Stretch out, clog streets

Summer: tattoos galore
& gourmet goodies
Fill farmers' markets

It's hot, no fog today
Of course we miss it
But no one notices

HURRICANE HARVEY

Somewhere the world is drying out,
Somewhere else it's still flooding,
Gotta start over again—a tired voice
On the radio, slow gulf-coast grammar....

Somewhere someone's trying to go home,
Somewhere else home is simply gone,
Somewhere the sky is a deep dark blue,
Somewhere else it's smoky from fires....

Daily disasters—natural disasters they say
But maybe not. We are the disaster,
An unnatural disaster & not just somewhere,

But damn near everywhere. What next?
What will we do next? More to the point:
What won't we do, while there's still time?

SUNDAY EVENING MUSIC

Full moon, thin clouds, following a slow trail of notes
Across a high desert evening. Is it really Schumann, or. . . .
Does it matter? Each separate sound, so many first stars,
Sonic bread crumbs scattered across this twilight sky. . . .

Ghost concert, echoing through cyberspace—what's that?
Where's that? Evening cloudburst's over now, just in time.
Quiet again. Quiet music. Quiet life, just out of reach, but
Almost here. We love these musical parentheses, pauses

In the non-stop roller coaster of the day-to-day, drumbeat
Of sour spirit and spite, poison politics, noise, nonsense.
Sunday slips quietly into yesterday with gentle music.

Requiem for a restless week, ransomed by internet radio,
Where do we fit into tomorrow? And this slow tide of music,
Where is it taking us? How can it resolve so much discord?

COYOTE SONGS

Coyotes calling other coyotes, purple evening sounds,
yelps and yips, long drawn-out howls, stereo echoes,
singing a song we don't know, don't even recognize
that makes us stop, look west, wonder what's next,

wonder why we think these evening thoughts—can't stop—
wonder and worry about what'll happen tomorrow.
The coyotes don't care, should we? We do and it isn't easy.
Shadow peaks tower over our thoughts, backstop them,

14,000 feet of dark rock and high drama, sky's edge,
the last snow's melted now, even in the highest gullies,
soon enough it will stage a comeback, we're ready,

but only for snow, nothing else, and there's so much else
that we didn't see coming, can hardly believe,
don't want to accept. Coyotes howling, evening music.

SUNSET

This infinite sky, ten minutes after sunset, too big,
Or maybe just big enough, but immense, grey-blue-pink,
Pastel smudges of cloud, finger painting of gods
That don't really exist but would if they could. . . .

It starts, it never stops, it doesn't finish, it's forever.
Evenings are forever here in the West, color lingers,
Endless hours, we try to remember what we wanted—
Wanted to see, wanted to do, can't remember. No use.

No use saying tomorrow will be a better day, it won't.
But it will be our tomorrow, and soon enough, our today.
We made it, let's enjoy it, under this vast empty-full sky.

Looking west: nothing between us and the horizon but
A 50-mile shadow of chamisa, yucca, cactus—these dark
Rabbit-brush brush strokes—tonight only the sky is bright.

EVENING IN THE SOUTH

Watching the falcons fly off,
Spread their wings, dive off the cliff. . . .
What were they waiting for?
What are we waiting for? . . .

To the west, over the ice field,
Voracious clouds devour sunset,
Can't complain: admire a faint pink
At the edges of scattered clouds.

Slight color better than no color,
Slight is enough. Careful!
Don't ask for too much, although

That's what we have here, tonight,
Night after night, beauty to spare,
As though it would last forever.

SMALL BIRDS

Swifts or swallows? Tiny dark arrowheads
Scribbling dotted lines across the sky,
At hyperspeed, 180-degree turns, & back,
In the blink of the eye. Don't blink. Clap!

They have their own way with the sky,
Not quiet motionless wide-winged soarers,
Not condors, not black-headed *jote* vultures
But every bit as at home in the air.

We wake and look out the window,
Across our lake, over peaks and glaciers,
And wait for the big birds to arrive. . . .

But these speed demons are already here,
Here & there, there, there, zigging and zagging,
Why slow down? Why not just fly…and fly.

MORNING SONNET WITH LONG LINES

Six-o'clock sun pushing through dark clouds clogging the eastern sky,
Slipping through, racing west to light signal fires on snowy summits,
Sending messages for us to decode: another day for us to define
By what we do, and don't do, and try to do, and sometimes succeed...

Nothing has changed, nothing's disappeared overnight, our lake's still there,
A wide bluish grey, looking for yesterday's blue, not yesterday's blues.
It's coming. The world rubs its eyes and wakes up, colors come slowly back,
Somewhere people are happy, all it takes is sunlight breaking through. . . .

Or a little good news on the internet, baffling blend of here and far-away,
We've almost forgotten what good news feels like, instead we have morning,
It'll do. Peeling back darkness in shadowy strips, pushing day's door wide.

Lost lake among half forgotten peaks, borrowing blue from the sky,
Giving it back with interest. Sunlight saves the day—a manner of speaking—
But why are we speaking? The day was never in danger. We are.

REMEMBERING A TRIP TO GALVESTON

Riding the Gulf Freeway's traffic tide, phone in hand:
Long freeway conveyor belt moving smoothly past us,
Back toward Houston, as we pretend to move forward,
No traffic noise, no noise at all, the AC purrs out cold,

Safe inside our steel bubble, outside, 90/90 humidity & temp,
Suffocatingly hot, outside, this endless passing parade:
Parking lots, car dealers, self-storage barracks,
Things and more things, dollar stores to buy still more,

Sideways shuffle from wanted to unwanted, wished for
And fast forgotten, greedily grasped, easily thrown away,
Because, hey, that's what we do, isn't it? New pickups,

New TVs, new phones, new apps, just don't ask why,
Too late for that, fingers tapping, typing with two thumbs:
I'm here, you're there. Great! I'll check in. Keep typing. . . .

TEMPUS FUGIT

The puzzle of passing time
Days pass, years pass
Nothing changes, still
Everything changes

We can't see it, feel it,
But we wake up one day
And there it is: a world
We aren't ready for

Didn't see coming
Caught us off guard
Stopped by a new now

Stopped cold—
What the hell! How
Did this ever happen?

LOOKING AHEAD

Tonight, no more answers, tonight, too tired
To start over, tomorrow, maybe, we'll see,
Maybe not, we'll either see or we won't. What's
Going to happen? Why bother? Why care?

Lots of reasons: start with the simplest, you,
Right here beside me, looking for good dreams,
Anyway, trying to sleep, ready to leap up at 6
In search of first light, addicted to beauty.

You make things simple in a complex world.
Dinner conversation in a spiraling circle— How?
How do we rethink capitalism? No idea.

But it needs doing, Why? Don't say why not?
The world has lost its connection with the future,
You are my connection to yesterday & tomorrow.

PROGRESS

Progress—just isn't what it used to be,
& maybe never was, not quite a hoax
But close, a rallying cry gone wrong.
Who believes in progress nowadays?

Falling off the edge of a slippery metaphor,
Looking for a new one—still looking—
Something that makes sense, a new picture
Of a new world, looking for tomorrow,

For a future we can live with, believe in
Instead of sliding backward, downhill. . . .
Easier to destroy than create, sure,

We knew that, but still we weren't ready—
For this great unwinding. How much time?
How much left? How will we spend it?

SUMMER IN THE SOUTH

Racing toward the solstice, night after night,
Days stretched to their limit, and beyond
Longer than days are meant to be, almost
Endless, but everything ends. We know that.

And try so hard to forget it, and never can.
The illusion of forever hangs in the air,
Stretches out across this vast calm lake,
Answers our questions before we ask them.

Summer in the south is a play without a plot,
Here for a long run, no end in sight, but soon
The globe tilts, autumn starts its slow creep.

We are here for the duration, never knowing
How long that is. Does it even matter?
Each day counts, solstice or not, already there.

THE DAILY

Drumbeat of bad news,
Din of other shoes dropping
Real news reporting
On fake democracy

Can't get worse, we say,
And it does, daily.
How did this happen?
We ask & already know,

The answer isn't pretty:
Turns out the bad guys
Work harder, longer

30, 40 years scheming,
Stifling, suppressing,
Subverting, till it's too late.

POETRY—WHY BOTHER?

Black marks on a white screen, ink on parchment,
It's all the same, signs equal sound equals sense,
Or sometimes nonsense, but worth it anyway. . .
Our poems, our attempts to say something

So directly that it can't, won't, be misunderstood.
What does it take? to reach someone? To get through?
I think it takes a lot of luck, having good readers
Makes us into good writers—this time around. . . .

But there won't be any other time, will there?
That's it, time's short, and each poem a short cut,
Some get there faster than a long argument,

Some never quite get there, it doesn't really matter,
Always an adventure, trying to compress life
Into a few lines, what could be harder, or better?

VISITORS

Outside, on the terrace, birds, two families of birds:
Black-headed vultures, *jotes*, heads & feathers inky dark,
And falcons, *caranchos*, jaunty black-feathered berets.
Orange beaks. Their *pater familias* has only one leg, Stumpy

We call him. He doesn't know or care what we call him,
It's a term of affection, but affection doesn't count.
What does? Only actions, deeds not desires, work
Not wishes, and Stump's a hard-working bird. Has to be.

We don't have to work that hard but maybe we should.
And would, if we knew what we really had to do.
How do they know? this flight of falcons, huddle of jotes?

These two tribes, feathered foes, or friends, flying in
Flying off again, balancing on one leg against the wind
Always waiting—for what? Do they know, do they care?

SLIPPING AWAY

The illusion of permanence
Didn't the Buddha warn us?
We're not as real as we think
As solid, unchanging, lasting

The world around us too
Not so solid not so safe
Here today and poof, gone
Was it real? Is it real?

The way things are
If, in fact, they really are
Fragile at best

Wake up and blink—
It's all gone, tomorrow
Won't be just another today

STORMY PATAGONIAN NIGHT

Such a wild stormy Patagonian night
The *Laura* tree outside our window
Shuddering & shaking, not just trembling
Late sun prying apart a few clouds

We wouldn't be anywhere else
The power is out again—last night
It didn't come back on till midnight—
Cheli and his son are out there, working

To turn the lights back on, two local linemen
Two hard working Patagones & their pickup
Full of tools & ladders, holding back the tide

Before long the lights will really go out
We won't be ready, never are, we'll pretend
To be shocked, but we know better

JOANN

Joann—a small person beneath a large hat,
A large hat and a larger smile, a warm heart,
And always a warm hug with open arms,
A small person filling a large space in our life.

Joann—ready to get on the motorcycle and go,
Ready for a new adventure—did you get enough?
Did you and John have enough adventures?
Enough time? No one does. But you got your share.

Joann—we're going to miss you, Crestone will miss you,
Patagonia's going to miss you, the lake, your cabin,
Your friends, even your jigsaw puzzles will miss you.

But you'll be there, in the sounds of John's guitar,
In the toasts and clinking of glasses around the table.
We'll keep you safely with us, under these mountains. . . .

MESSAGES & DEVICES

Sent with two thumbs, *von meinem iPad gesendet*,
Messages crisscrossing through cyberspace, back
& forth, more & more, every day, as if they mattered.
Maybe they do, I doubt it. How much can you share?

How much do you really want, or need, to share?
Take your time. "When the deer is ready to be killed
It will come into the forest," did the Buddha say that?
Really? Messages pour in, we aren't ready, don't care

But answer anyway, with fewer words, fewer & fewer,
It's a code: I'm here, you're there. OK. Start over. . . .
It's what we do: *texto ergo sum*, or so we hope.

But it isn't true. What if we have nothing, or almost nothing
To say, are we really here? have we really lived? isn't that
The goal: live a life worth sharing, in words, in person? . . .

SOUTHERN SUMMER SOLSTICE 2017

This grey wet evening, low clouds, impossible
To see across the lake, a soft grey screen
Hiding blue water and darker blue peaks
That aren't there, solstice sun sound asleep. . .

No hurry to light up this landscape, not tonight,
Invisible is just as beautiful as what's visible
The faintest line between lake and sky, real? unreal?
Doesn't matter, but it feels right, so much emptiness,

But still full, full of space, full of time,
No hurry, this is Patagonia, clocks slow down
Calendar pages don't turn but seasons fly by

And here we are, tonight, at the top of the year
Refugees from a frightening future, almost ready
For that long slide, downhill, toward winter

HERE IN THE SOUTH

These long, almost too long days
Extra hours—starting dinner at 9:30—
Time stretched thin, but still full,
Almost another life, an extra life

These hours add up, do we feel it?
Appreciate it? all this extra time?
50% more hours, 50% more beauty?
I doubt it, but I'll take it if I find it.

And it's all around: southern sunsets
Go on...and on...and on, a falcon family
Flies lazy figure eights in a high wind

Marble bluffs shine in the last light. . .
How did we get here? How long
Can it last? We'll use each extra hour.

JANUARY 1 IN CHILE

Feliz año, happy (new) year, or
Happy (any) year, Happy Year!
Only in Chile—saving a syllable
Slippery language full of short cuts

Why say more than you need to
And how much is that & to whom
Instead of punctuation, a smile,
Igualmente—same to you, enough

Do they mean it Do we mean it
Do we know what we really mean
Do we even want to know. Perhaps

Wishes are good but never enough
The next step is making it so, 365
Days, happy or not, here we go. . . .

Casa Mármol, 1 Jan 2018

AFTERNOON IN THE SOUTH

Soaring silent a black vulture
Glides by, then out over the lake
Sunshine is a weight on the skin
Clouds only a morning memory

Ice field peaks shine with snow melt
No wind today, dreaming of waves
The lake's endless blue stays quiet
While nature holds its breath

Shadows stretch slowly east
Nothing hurries, nothing moves
Almost nothing, maybe clock hands

Ticking quietly toward evening—
Another day far from power & spite
Far away from racism & resistance

TRUMP YEARS #2   (WITH CHILDISH RHYMES)

Year two, what can we do? We? How about me?
What the hell! Time will tell, but it won't tell much
All the king's horses and all the king's men
Couldn't put our country back together again

There is no king, no horses, no men, no wall—
Not yet, it wasn't Humpty Dumpty that fell, just a fall,
That's all, a fall from grace—wasn't that much grace
To start with, but we dreamed of a better place

And we haven't given up but the dream is dimmer.
No, there's no king yet either, but the shadow's there
Floating above everything, floating in the air, where

Instead of building, rebuilding is all we can hope to do
And it won't be easy, reconstruction never is, what's new?
What the hell, we have no choice, let's go. How about you?

Eine kleine Nachtmusik

This baby owl, no, just a young one, not a baby
Trotting from window to window on its white feet
Eating moths—it's autumn, the moths are here.
For how much longer? not long, too cold now,

Frost on the windshield in the morning, and snow,
New snow on all the peaks, it's not melting
As it should. Tomorrow's the equinox: a moment
Of balance before we tip downhill, already sliding

Toward winter. Winter can't wait, but we can,
No hurry to bundle up, light the stove, bank the fire
Toward morning, toward what? We're never ready

But we'll cope, tell each other how beautiful it is.
And it really is. Life on the lake, a quiet adventure—
We didn't choose it, it chose us, we accept.

GUILTY?

What to do? How many choices?
Spectator or actor? Start there.
We're all spectators now, the internet
Lets us watch what we'll never see

And maybe don't want to see,
Buried in bad news, powerless,
Or so it feels, to change anything,
Just spectators, maybe just voyeurs?

The globalization of bread & circuses:
Christians & lions, school kids & shooters,
As long as it's someone else. . . .

So, spectator or actor? No choice—
Start pushing, try to set things straight
Or bear the blame, share the guilt.

AUTUMN EVENING IN THE FAR SOUTH

9:30, it's been dark for hours, winter closing in,
Seems like only yesterday the light was endless.
It wasn't, but then, nothing is. Not this year,
Not ever, even so, summer left in a hurry. . .

Snow line dropping, temperatures too, too fast—
Not really too fast, we just aren't ready, never are.
A question I remember from forty years ago:
Are you ready to be ready? Maybe not yet.

No use waiting for beauty, standing in line,
It has to be an ambush, and it is, every time.
Can't find beauty on the calendar, don't even try.

Just look, just see, just say yes—at least say OK.
And where'd all that lost light go? Fled with summer,
North across the equator, lighting other evenings. . . .

CARANCHOS

These two birds look so cold,
Feathers fluffed out and fluttering
In the afternoon wind, while
Raindrops spatter on the stone.

Windswept slate terrace, a ledge
Dropping off into pure space:
Clouds & peaks & more clouds,
Room to soar in the worst weather.

Our two falcons, *caracara caranchos*,
Dive into the sky whenever they want,
Easier to take off than land, or stand,

Motionless facing into the wind.
What are they waiting for? Maybe
They aren't really waiting, they just are.

AUTUMN MEMORIES

Ragged snow-plastered peaks
Scraping the bottom of clouds
Patchwork mix of autumn colors
A riot of reds, some leftover green

Storms roll through, scrub
Everything back to zero
Mist hugs the lake, soon enough
Torn away by ice-field winds

The picture's never the same
Can't wait to open our eyes
Even today, waking to rain

Autumn rain, steady & cold
Autumn days passing too fast
Autumn memories safely stored

AUTUMN IMPERFECTION

Autumn drags on, wet day after wet day,
Dark clouds take turns blocking the sun,
Swallowing the golden light, first drizzle,
Then rain, even rainbows look tired—we are.

Autumn's just a possibility not a promise,
You never know, an overnight wind
Can strip the leaves from a whole forest—
A lesson in impermanence we never learn

Or maybe keep learning, year after year,
A long goodbye, gathering colors for winter,
Warming hands & heart on the year's embers,

Autumn doesn't need us, but we need it
Or think we do. Would it be as beautiful
If we didn't care so much, love it so much?

SAN LUIS SUMMER

The mercury is boiling, not really, but damn near
The hills are burning, not here, but just out of sight
The sky opaque with smoke & haze, where's the blue?
Record heat in Denver, 105 degrees—mountain weather?

The new normal, or simply the permanent new anormal?
I think so. Wildfires have burned up the cell phone towers.
No internet in Salida, our "big city." *Cash Only* signs
On business doors, no credit cards, or even phone today.

Seventy thousand acres black, two hundred houses gone,
In Washington, a few more presidential temper tantrums,
A few more NATO allies insulted, Obama rules rolled back.

What's next? We wait for rain, get only virga, raindrops
That never reach the ground, evaporate, leave gray streaks
On smoky grey air. A scorching scary summer, barely begun.

3 July 2018

KCSM, THE BAY AREA'S JAZZ OASIS

Portraits in Space and Time, just another title
Of another jazz CD—why not? Portraits
Of people we know, or ought to know,
But don't. Sound pictures, echoing

Around an already dark house—why not?
Clear clarinet and strident sax. I get it
But I really don't. Basso rumble of
Hammond B3, a summer thunderstorm.

Tomorrow we'll wake to dry parched earth.
What will change? Everything. And nothing.
Wilbur Little solos on a Duke Jordan tune.

"Go forth and do good"—the DJ exhorts us.
But it isn't that easy. You have to want to,
And so many don't, *tout le contraire*.

CRESTONE EVENING

Another sunset, how many more?
Clouds turn pink, peach, crimson,
Autumn is sneaking up on us
With yellow snakeweed, purple aster,

Wild hares masquerading as cottontails
Streak off through the chamisa, leap
Over cactus, dive into shadow burrows,
Soon shadows will own everything.

Soon enough it will be over—can't wait,
But we will. Soon enough we'll be over too
And for that we'll gladly wait. No hurry.

Each sunset's a gift, each new season
Another treasure, and autumn's best of all.
Tomorrow the world turns to gold.

QUANTUM GRAVITY

OK, nothing is as it seems—what's the difference,
Between a cloud of probabilities & a cloud of illusions?
We are surrounded by questions, conundrums, confusions.
Hard enough just to figure out this everyday here-and-now,

See it for what it is, and isn't. Do we need to look deeper?
Really? Nice to know, I suppose, that infinity isn't needed,
And doesn't make sense, that the world is granular,
That time's a fiction. But it feels so real. Entropy feels real.

And it is, underneath all the math: the world cooling down,
Growing older, like us, year after year, dragging us on
Toward a last farewell. Isn't that a good enough definition?

Time is loss. Solve those equations, measure it, and then
Mourn it. At a point (almost) time stops, disappears.
A single quantum of love can cancel spacetime too.

THE NEW WELL

A new water well in a drought-dried landscape—
It's a lot to ask but we're asking, & waiting for answers,
Day after day, a stack of half-rusty, half-shiny metal
Looms up in the driveway, diesel motor growling,

And we look on baffled. What's happening? What's
Gonna happen next? We don't know, can't even guess.
Drilling a well through an overgrown sand dune isn't easy,
Prehistoric technology, the worn-out machinery protests

But keeps on drilling. Life imitates art, imitates the blues:
You don't miss your water till your well runs dry, Damn!
Feels like the future—too many straws in the aquifer

But here we are, under the mountain, getting first gulps
Unpolluted, from an underground river, almost as if
We deserved it, almost an addiction, almost enough.

TOO TOO

Too little, too much, too late, too soon
Too many people, cars, cares, crises,
Not enough room but too much money,
Then all at once, too little—never enough,

Never just enough, never just right,
Often just wrong, too much too wrong—
Much too much, and too hard to fix
Too many moving parts, sometimes too few,

Too many believers, too many opinions,
Not enough facts, not enough evidence
Or too much to take in, to understand

Too many problems, not enough answers
Too many levers of power in too few hands
Too much, too little, always the same story.

SPACETIME

Spacetime? a literary fiction? or science fiction?
We have trouble putting the two together,
Einstein didn't, but that doesn't help us
To solve the same puzzle. We read the story

And pretend we understand it, we don't.
Space goes on and on, will always be there,
But we stop, and time stops with us, it's over
As soon as we are, actually way too soon.

We are our own yardsticks, our own clocks,
Not very accurate, easy to read, easy to believe,
Dreaming of forever, but measuring only today.

Spacetime is poetry, puzzle, dream, and myth,
A fantasy that's been proved real, again & again,
By measurements we can't begin to understand.

THEY SAY...

There's no straight line in nature — wrong.
We look across the lake, at a pale blue line,
Horizon-straight and perfect — marks the end
Of something, the start of something else,

Cuts the world in half, above the line
Mountains are gnarled, snow-plastered,
Rocky blisters on the planet's skin, below
Lies our lake, tabletop flat, robins-egg blue.

Lines, flat planes, OK, how about right angles?
They're out there too, a natural geometry,
Crystals bending light into color. It's all there

If we look for it—and even if we don't.
Doesn't matter what they say, or who says it.
So what really does matter? We're still asking.

A BUSY SKY

A busy sky, the clouds are in a hurry this morning,
Rainbows have to run to keep up, they don't stop,
Caracara falcons blow by, struggling to land,
Wings wide, lighter than air, tossed by the wind,

Doors rattle, roofs bang, the chimney pipe echoes,
Out on the lake whitecaps move even faster,
Maitén trees never stop shaking, bend don't break,
Through the clouds snow appears, then disappears.

What next? clearing skies? random raindrops? summer?
Or not? The daily drama of a pure Patagonian sky
At war with itself, changing faster than we can follow.

A busy Patagonian day where nothing has to happen
And doesn't. Morning's long race toward evening, light
Pushing against dark clouds, peeling them slowly away.

TRUE STORIES

True stories are usually tragedies
Happy endings usually hype:
fiction and fantasy. Who's innocent
When almost everyone is guilty?

But guilty of what? Not caring,
Or not caring enough to do something,
Do anything. What did the poet say?
To take arms against a sea of troubles,

And by opposing end them. . . As if we could,
What if we can but won't? That's tragedy.
What if we could get started? What if? . . .

Life is catching up to us, we can't run away.
The future—tomorrow—tightening the screws
On today. So who's innocent? Not us.

NOT OPTIMISTIC

for Tom Butler

"I'm not optimistic but I'm hopeful," —Tom,
What the hell do you mean by that?
Well, I guess I know, but I'm not so sure. . .
Time to slow down and define just what it is

That we are afraid will happen, what might,
Or might not, be the last chapter of the story.
It isn't a good story, but it's a rich one,
Enough beauty, grace and grit to bet on.

Is that all? Is the future nothing more than a bet?
& what are the odds? Not clear, but it's a bad bet.
The stakes aren't really that high, yes, you bet your life,

But it's only one life. The world won't even notice,
Keeps on changing. So what the hell are we hoping for?
Don't know. But don't stop. Hopeful, not optimistic.

WINTER

We wait for winter.
Winter waits for snow.
Winter hides its ransom notes
under frozen puddles

Winter sends us snowflake messengers
with made-up news
of a whiter country.
We used to believe them.

Now we're no longer sure.
We want proof.
Winter is camped out

just up the pass,
Just out of sight,
over there somewhere. .

TOMORROW, HERE

The wide, blank, blue canvas of our lake
Waiting for the wind's broad brush strokes,
A quiet evening, storm clouds disappearing,
Soft light growing ever softer, the white rim

Of snowy peaks painting a zigzag horizon.
Late light, last light, how long can it last?
It's already nine, ten, still light, still more light,
It never stops. Why should it? But we will.

Don't fret. This one evening is enough,
It's already more than we bargained for,
Than we deserve. And who deserves what?

Who dealt these cards? We'll never know.
Why are we here? Right now? Tomorrow
We'll still be here, still asking the same questions.

QUIET EVENING, LAGO CHELENKO

Last light lingers, gilds western peaks
no wind tonight, the lake is layered
with blue-on-blue stripes, ruffled reflections
blue-grey at first, more color still to come

Evening here is a long story with no plot
never ends the same way, never ends at all
never disappoints, never lets us look away
last light lasts and lasts, won't say goodbye

neither will we, this is where we belong
as glaciers turn softly pink—pastel Patagonia—
and two tired falcons soar off to their nest

Another day without any real answers
to any real questions, these days so much more
than just check marks on our endless to-do list

SUNSET UNDER STACKED LENTICULARS

Clouds twisted like pretzels, lit up like neon tubes
Just another sunset spectacle, right on time,
As wind off the ice fields blows the banked coals
Of a Patagonian day back to life, brighter & redder,

A sky finally on fire, burning up, not burning out,
Dress rehearsal for a psychedelic solstice, 9:45,
Night still hours away, & dinner cold on the stove,
Doesn't matter—another day tiptoes off stage. . . .

What can we do with so much strange beauty?
Drunk on sunset & wine, but only one glass,
Hard to take it all in, hard to keep breathing,

Hard to remember how we got here, & when,
We know skies like this are forever, but we aren't.
Better gather them up for winter—soon enough.

MOTHER-OF-PEARL

Looking at the lake this evening I think mother-of-pearl,
and then think again, what the hell does that mean? And
then realize it doesn't matter—just words. Shiny, shimmering,
soft and subtle colors swimming together, sliding together,

It's only water, but water never looked this good, or else
we never looked at it this way, from this condor's aerie,
this landing in the sky, marble ledge above the lake that
caracaras and *jotes*, falcons and vultures, call their own.

Us too, we call this lake our own, although it isn't,
It's captured us for sure, our attention and our hearts.
We're invisible, tiny dots on top of a marble cliff,

Overlooking space, waiting for wind to break the spell.
Tonight, there's just enough wind for the birds to soar,
Not enough to wrinkle the pearl grey skin of the lake.

PAST LIVES

Who was that person I remember being?
How did he get there? Where was he going?
Not here, but here I am. And where to, now?
Can't even guess, not sure I want to know.

Although of course, I do know. We all do.
But that long-ago me—what the hell,
How did I even survive? Less obvious,
Adventure at all costs, it didn't cost a penny.

I climbed routes that were too hard for me,
Borrowed another life, tried it on, just to see—
See how it felt, see what I could make

Of another hand, dealt by accident:
Other lives, other loves, other memories,
Not really mine, although I lived them all.

SOLSTICE DECEMBER 21, 2018

The year turns over, in the north it's turning upside down,
Here in the south a full moon rises into a new season—
A new summer—full of promise, full of peril, enough sun,
But never enough rain—the end of what? the start of what?

Back home—we used to call it home—the news is black,
An army of orcs disguised in suits, working overtime,
Spreading stress, we don't want to call it terror but it is,
Stealing babies, stealing Christmas, they don't care.

Do we? Of course we do, but what are we willing to do?
Tomorrow we'll have a little less light but won't feel it,
And a little less life to live, we won't feel that either,

And more to do while we can. Who knows for how long?
The earth will keep spinning, the seasons keep changing,
Tipping points of all sorts will tip and pass. And we will too

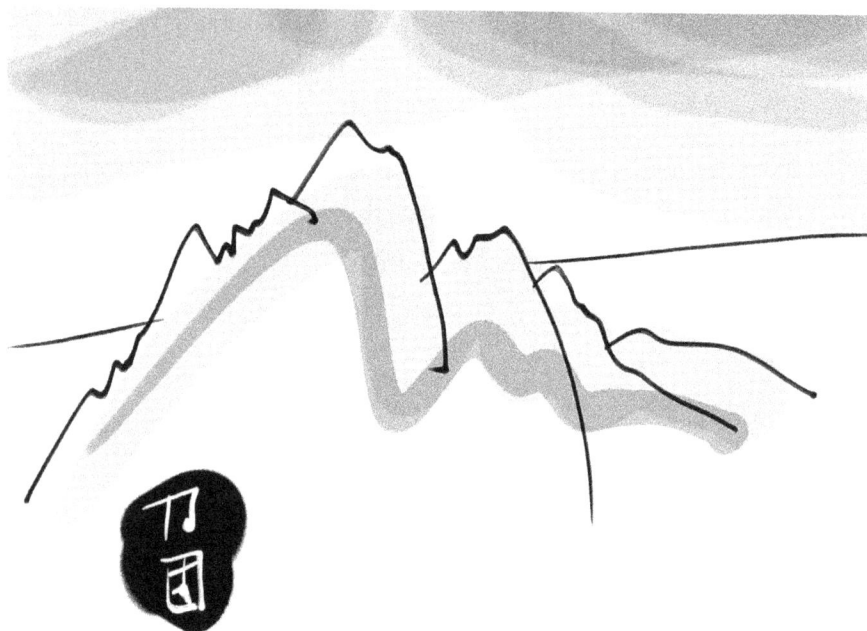

2019
STILL MORE
SONNETS

THE SLOT MACHINE OF TIME

The years spin by, non-stop, then suddenly pause,
Seventy-five—jackpot! you win, I win, we win,
How is it possible that your eyes have grown brighter,
Your smile warmer, your heart bigger, and your lover

Madder than ever about you? The way it should be
And almost never is. Tonight love is better than luck.
Those numbers don't add up, don't mean very much,
But your smile means everything, everything good.

The years tell one story, but we don't believe it,
Why should we? We aren't tired, bored, discouraged.
Maybe we haven't grown up yet. Why should we?

Every morning I'm surprised to wake up next to you,
Such a beautiful girl, such a fierce artist, to rediscover
How much I love you, what an adventure it is.

3 Jan 2019

TOMORROW, TODAY

Patagonia is burning, but mostly out of sight
The Atacama desert is washing away
But it's mostly empty—do deserts matter?
The gods are angry—do they even exist?

Does it really matter? What does? Our world
Fraying at the edges, and soon at the center
Does anyone care? Are we capable of caring?
Apparently not—nothing matters till it hurts

Can we imagine what's about to happen? No
It is already happening and we can't see it
For us tomorrow looks like today—it won't be

Time to get ready—but ready for what exactly?
A life we didn't ask for in a world we didn't want?
We'll do the best we can—we know it won't work

EVERYDAY WORLD

The devil's in the details, the petty private details
Of our passionate personal lives—all we've got,
Not really enough but still, much too much
Just to ignore, to look beyond, to even try to—

No use—we can't ever see beyond ourselves,
Can't imagine a world without us on center stage
Surrounded by all our familiar props
Playing our familiar roles, mouthing familiar lines,

The never-changing normal of daily life,
Not that life is really so predictable, maybe
We just lack the imagination to see what's new.

We know soon enough everything will be new,
But will we even notice? Maybe the new normal
Won't feel new at all. Maybe we're just stuck.

WAKING UP

Waking up to the illusion of forever,
Trapped between short horizons,
Today, tomorrow, yesterday, this now
That seems suspended, timeless,

And doesn't let us feel the future,
That warmer future coming soon,
Soon enough, even if we can't see it
Believe it, make ourselves care.

These mountains look like forever,
This sky promises us blue forever.
We're kidding ourselves, we can't help it,

We know better, today's illusion
Is almost gone. And it was a good one,
The world felt like forever—it wasn't.

COUNTDOWN

… to what? tomorrow? next year?
a future we don't want to think about?
a future we can't stop thinking about?
maybe just counting: hours, days, years, lives?

everything counts, what I did today, or didn't,
what I'll do tomorrow, or maybe won't do
or won't have enough time to ever do,
life's a countdown and time is running out

but we'll get there, wherever, whenever,
whatever *there* is…. I can guess,
I think it's where we don't want to be,

time was always elastic, stretching ahead,
but now we can see the end—of something,
of a lot—suddenly the countdown's all too real.

HOMELESS

Ragged vets on freeway on-ramps
"Willing to work—god bless"
Honor students sleeping in cars
Kids in cages at the border

A whole town burned down
More wildfires on the way
Water up to the second floor
And no flood insurance

Bay Area homelessness
Exploding year-on-year
It didn't used to be like this

How many homeless?
70 million refugees today
Soon, people without a planet

INERTIA

Today is just like yesterday, nothing changes
Maybe the to-do list gets a little longer, maybe not
But it feels about the same, although it really isn't
Hard to tell that the water in our pot is heating up

Easy not to notice, so much else to think about,
To take care of, small daily dramas, or big ones,
Like always, like growing up, like paying the bills
Like cleaning the gutters, planning that vacation

Hell, you earned it, no need to change, no time
To rethink things, rethink anything, to get ready
For what's next, those scary stories in the Guardian

Drive downtown, everything looks about the same,
Just a little more crowded, a little more expensive
No time, no need to hop out of this simmering pot

TWO SONNETS, TWO WAYS. . .

1

Questions without answers
What questions? Who's asking?
We already know the answers
And they aren't good. Are they?

Todays without tomorrows
That doesn't sound right
But we know it's true
Kids without a future, at least

Not the future they want
That we all wanted, still want
And can no longer imagine

When did we give up, and why?
Fighting feels good, not each other
But this future nobody wants

2

Preguntas sin respuestas
¿Qué preguntas?
¿Y quién está preguntando?
Todo el mundo y nadie

¿Qué queremos aprender
Que ya no sabemos?
¿El origen de los problemas
De las tragedias de hoy?

¿Las soluciones? Cierto
Pero tendremos que
Encontrar nuevas preguntas

Y encontrar el coraje
De creer las respuestas
¿Por qué no? ¡Por qué sí!

NO

No— our best answer
To tomorrow, to today
To the unacceptable
What else can we say?

No's enough, unambiguous
Direct, it's not just negative
No can be a verb: refusing
To go along, accept, support

No is the only right answer
To cruelty, unfairness, brutality
To greed & the cult of money

Right answer to wrong choices
Right reply to too much power
Yes, no can mean yes

FUTURE TENSE

Looking for the future—a future, any future—
Without finding it, lost in an improbable present
We wouldn't have wished for, & didn't choose,
That maybe isn't real, a nonexistent now.

Still, here we are, here, but not exactly ready
For tomorrow, not totally finished with yesterday.
It never ends, this regret for a world of lies,
For the pattern we see in passing days.

No use looking any further—looking for what?
Reasons, motives, explanations, something else…
No need even to imagine a different future…

The future is busy imagining us. We aren't
Strong enough to defy its pattern, resist its pull.
The future creates us. Not the other way round.

THE VISITOR

A *jote* floats down from the stormy sky, motionless,
Not a feather moves, not one wing beat,
A black headed vulture, *jote de cabeza negra*,
Lands on a boulder, stands facing into the wind,

And stands, and stands, as motionless on its rock
As in soaring flight, head turns slightly right, left,
Then back into the wind . . . waiting? For what?
Who knows? Just waiting, waiting for nothing,

Finally spreads black wings, tilts, slides off into space,
Economy of movement, economy of non-movement,
Soaring somewhere beneath us, against the cliff.

We're waiting too. And who knows for what?
Maybe tomorrow? Not for an unlikely day with no wind?
Maybe Patagonia is what we've always been waiting for

AN OLD STORY

An old story, an old struggle, the haves and have nots.
Who wins? Nobody. Who cares? Damn near everybody.
But not in the same way, not about the same things.
Wanting more, giving less: ask, take, refuse, protect.

An old story without a happy ending, but all stories end.
This one too. What is it the haves have? Money or things?
Is there even a difference? What do the have nots want?
Just the same, but what do they—all of us really—need?

A future. What we all need, and see slipping away,
Day by day, a livable planet, a planet we can call home.
We thought we were telling this story, but we aren't.

The earth gets to write the ending now, we had our turn,
And yes, we blew it, the haves and have nots will go on
Fighting, asking for more and more, getting less and less.

LIVING IN A CHINESE CURSE

Yes, these are "interesting times," too interesting,
But never boring, change comes fast and furious,
Certainties grow less certain, guess they never were,
Take one step forward, slide two steps back, repeat.

History happened so long ago: dates and dynasties,
Long lists in history books—where else?—we'd read,
Repeat, recite, then quickly forget, but this is different,
Now we're watching history unfold, maybe unravel.

50 years of progress wiped out with the stroke of a pen,
Is this revenge? By whom? against whom? and why?
And was it really progress? We had more choices

Or maybe just more things.... maybe way too many.
Those history books never told us the real story
But we believed them, now we're slamming them shut.

AUTUMNAL EQUINOX

a day like any other
earth spinning underfoot
sun circling overhead
calendar says it's autumn

doesn't feel any different
autumn will get here eventually
we'll say goodbye to summer
say Wow and act surprised

meanwhile we wait for a sign
something to celebrate,
to say Just in time

we're tired of summer
want to pull out sweaters
we wish fall would hurry up

30 March 2019
in Patagonia

THANKSGIVING 2019

No longer just reading history but living it
Watching, waiting for the next act, tomorrow—
So damn fast, history in high gear, and now
It will never slow down. The whole story,

Our story, is coming to an end, coming apart.
Nothing is certain, certainly not those certainties
We grew up with: a five-day, 40-hour, work week,
A pension when it's all done, a fictitious family:

Grandparents, grandkids, midcentury myths
That somehow made it into this new century,
Middle class, working class, & Thanksgiving dinners

As if we'll all be here next year. We won't. But
We'll surely be somewhere, no telling where,
Either making history, or being unmade by it.

28 Nov 2019

COUNTDOWN TO THE SOLSTICE

Days getting longer—are the clocks slowing down?
Or speeding up? Are we? Would we if we could?
Or are we stuck, motionless, as life rushes by
As the globe turns, as life turns, turns inside out?

Humankind, all of us, running out of excuses
As autumn runs out the clock, or here in the South
Spring races to send out new shoots and finish
Painting Patagonia green. The news is grim

With only occasional small flashes of hope—what next?
The amazon burning, Europe coming unglued,
The US almost written off, the mercury rising.

Whipsawed between the personal and the planetary
We look for signs, we say there is still time, 21 days
To go, and how many more solstices will we celebrate?

December 1st, 2019.

SUMMER SOLSTICE 2019

Solstice sends us out
Looking for metaphors
Something to say
We haven't already said

We think: this is important
But is it really? is it even real?
Really today, really tonight
And not next week?

How can we know?
How could we possibly
Tell this longest day

From any other
And why do we care?
Why should we?

CHRISTMAS IN THE SOUTH

Evening on a prow of rock pushing out into the southern sky
Above a lake crisscrossed by winds from three directions,
Wispy strands of *coirón* tossing along the border of our bluff,
The wild windblown hair of Patagonia dancing nonstop

Above *Isla Macias* a rainbow stretches up toward pure gray,
Somewhere west, over the icefield, sunlight is sneaking
Through clouds to light the marble cliffs beyond Puerto Cristal,
Over there, across the lake, our white-capped, wind tossed lake.

Last night was the big deal, Christmas Eve, *Noche Buena*.
Why did we eat only seafood? That's just the way it is. Nobody
Believes this story, nobody thinks baby Jesus will save us

But everyone enjoys the lights, the music, the gifts, the food.
We want to forget the wildfires, the politics, what's coming,
We want tomorrow to be as beautiful as today, as this Christmas.

25 December 2019

ALMOST 2020

Another year, it almost makes sense, the world waking up
Hoarding extra minutes of light every day, every evening
We take it on faith, won't feel it for another month or two
But there's light at the end of this tunnel called winter

Sunlight, the magnet pulling us around the turning year
Everything is turning now, turning round, turning upside down
A good picture, a comforting thought, not starting, not stopping
Just going round, the spinning seasons always offer another chance

How strange to write this in summer so far south of the equator
Everything's the opposite here, but still the same, the same sun
No longer pulling but pushing us forward toward a summer

That will get hotter and hotter even as the days get shorter
It almost makes sense, not quite, but we're just glad to be here
Riding this beautiful planet round and round in endless circles

30 Dec 2019

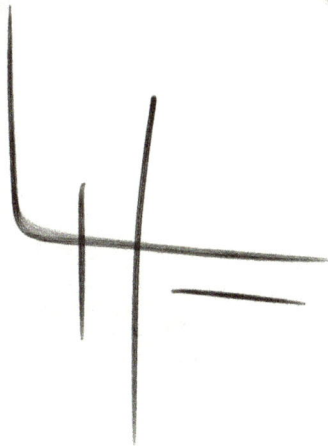

under mountains

2 0 2 0
FINALLY

GRETA

"No one is too small to make a difference."
No one too big to be held to account
No one too dumb to see where we're going
No one too clever to avoid what's coming.

What's the message then? Pay attention,
No one is exempt, we're all in this together?
No one gets a free pass, no one gets off?
Or is it something else, altogether different?

True, no one's too small to make a difference
But why do so few even try? They, no, actually we,
Can't imagine what we could possibly do—

Why not? not enough imagination? or just too selfish,
Too busy being busy, pretending it's all OK?
It isn't and we aren't. Pretending we don't care?

9 Jan 2020

THE LAKE TONIGHT

A midsummer storm has whitewashed the peaks again,
Snow down to timberline, even lower, where yesterday
It was all rock, sure, the glaciers are smaller than
Just ten years ago, but they're still pure white.

It was just a moment— clouds lifted, then fell,
The blue-grey pastel sketch of the lake
Asks us to imagine the far shore, through
A blanket of mist and wide-spaced raindrops,

The birds have flown back to their nests
On the cliff below us, *caracaras* and *jotes*,
Sharing our airspace, borrowing our wind.

Mist equals mystery, no need to see it all
But really, we can't even imagine a lake
More perfect than this one, out there, for real.

THESE TIMES

Making sense of nonsense
Not easy, not really possible
But that's where we are
Crazy isn't crazy any more

Doesn't matter if it's absurd
It can still work, and does
For now if not forever
For today, & one tomorrow

One more day clinging to facts
Looking for proof, trying to care
As we slide downhill ever faster

We read the papers like comics
Don't dare look past the headlines
Nothing makes sense any more

11 Jan 2020

THE LAST LAP

Not just a metaphor any more, it's real
Too real, no use saying we saw it coming
We didn't really, didn't believe it, now the smoke
From fires in Australia is here, and here

Can be anywhere, and anywhere is everywhere
Everything is burning, sometimes in slow motion
But still burning, the whole planet, we know
What's happening but we can't feel it, not yet

Tomorrow everything will be the same as always
But somehow different if we pay attention
Are we grown up enough to really pay attention?

Kids have no choice, they have to be brave
They know better than we do what we all want
A future we can believe in, a tomorrow we can trust.

9 Feb 2020

LAST POEM

What if this were my last poem? What could I say?
How could I start it? End it? Put my whole life in it?
I'd have to start with you, Linde, end with you too,
All the rest? Who cares? Loving you is the real story.

Poetry is a mixture of love and loss, what you refuse
To say goodbye to, or turn your back on, or forget,
What you remember, what matters, what you love—
Clouds and rain, sunshine and rainbows, a clearing wind

Birds wheeling overhead, seasons and their colors,
Morning coffee, faraway friends, quiet music,
Crazy adventures and close calls, red sunsets,

Falling in love, a big adventure, then staying in love,
The biggest adventure, finding the right person, maybe
Just luck, enough luck to fill a poem, or a whole life.

9 Feb 2020

GET WELL

for Art Goodtimes

Every time you opened your mouth
words tumbled out, poems or
proto-poems, thoughts working
to shape themselves into poems

So who needs a healthy throat?
We all do, poets more than most
even though poems will be heard
and loved, one way or another

Get well, Art, if you can, and even
if you can't, don't worry, those poems
will find their way to the right ears

What a stash you have given us
you and McRedeye, and all your
impossible paleohippie personas. . . .

19 Feb 2020

POLISHING THE MOUNTAIN

for John Reeves

Creation by subtraction, sculpture's puzzle
Not stacking stone but peeling it away
Three dimensions into two, flattening form
To find a new form, that was there all along

Polishing a marble mirror, imitating clouds
Some white, some gray, mixing, blending
Day by day above a lake bluer than the sky
And day by day the marble throws off its scales

No, John does this work, slicing, hammering
Chisel bites, blade buzzes, cuts and polishes
The stone becomes itself, becomes a floor

Actually much more, the heart of a house
A future house, on this marble point, this lookout over
Something endlessly changing, endlessly beautiful

21 Feb 2020

ANOTHER PASTEL EVENING

Another pastel evening, pulling the last color from a declining day
Sunset struggling to make itself noticed, but we'll always look—
Look out, look up, look around and ask why, why are we still here
When so many aren't? Soft pink streamers fill the spaces

Between mountains and a summer ceiling of ragged gray
Time to put away camera and tripod, open a bottle of wine,
Watch last light fade, watch first stars fill those gaps in the sky
Watch a quiet world grow even quieter, watch nothing happen

And enjoy it, nothing at all, nothing new tonight, not here,
Nature turns in and goes to sleep, as we will soon enough
Tomorrow is soon enough to read about stocks plunging

A pandemic spreading across the globe, growing inequality
And its growing pains and protests, we can wait and will
And tomorrow, here, will be just as beautiful as ever.

28 Feb 2020

ONE EVENING ON THE LAKE

So this is Patagonia
Is it even real?
Is it a trip into the past
Just before the world went nuts?

Doesn't always feel real.
Too simple, too clean,
Too perfect, too otherworldly
We worry it can't last

We worry we won't last
And we wont, but what
And who disappears first?

We pretend that this view
This watershed, these peaks
Will never change. We're wrong

5 March 2020

29 MARCH 2020

A bad month almost over, and more to come
A good day almost over, and more to come
On the terrace shadows are lengthening
The sun is chasing its own rays over the horizon
The lake says a long goodbye to the color blue
Maitén trees are dancing in the evening breeze
It's too easy here, on the other side of the globe
A friend's world has shrunk to a 4-meter balcony

We can't complain, and we won't, but we should
About our country, our politicians, our president
It's payback, in earlier times people like these
Bought and sold slaves, now they are bought
And sold into disgrace for their craven obedience
To money, to Putin, to Wall Street, we won't forgive them

29 march 2020

19 APRIL 2020

Almost four months into this new world disorder
Almost enough time, almost but not quite, to see
Where we are heading, what happened, & why
In this pandemic sweepstakes the US comes in last

Not last to take it seriously, because we haven't yet
But last and least effective in dealing with it
I remember what my friend Cado always said:
"If you don't deal with reality, reality will deal with you"

He was right, of course, and Trump was wrong
Still is, leading our confused country over a cliff
Looking for someone else to blame, someone to insult

Looking for love, for ratings, for four more years
To finish the job—so much destruction already
It's hard to believe things can get worse. They can.

NO ONE KNOWS, I

No one knows, that's the perfect answer
To the question of the moment: what now?
No one knows what's going to happen next
Tomorrow, next week, next month, next year

I suppose we can get used to such total
Uncertainty, but still it's a surprise.
We thought we knew, knew it all, and
We liked the future we thought we knew

Uncertainty is the new certainty, for now
And now is endless. What now? Can mean
What then? what someday? or mean nothing

No one knows— no ambiguity there, no one
Means no one, might mean me, you, them
All of us, uncertain, waiting for an answer

NO ONE KNOWS, II

No one knows—the perfect answer
To the most awkward question
What now? What next? No one knows.
Tomorrow or next week or next year....

Impossible to say, don't even try
We don't like so much uncertainty
But we had better get used to it
Uncertainty is the new certainty

No one knows when it will be over
When life will start up again
When we can go out again

Sit in a cafe and watch the crowd
Flow past, when we'll feel safe
Ordering dinner or hugging a friend

THE WAITING GAME

What are we waiting for, the all-clear?
To get up and go, and go where?
We're already there, here, right here
Where we'd choose to be if we could,

Or could have before we were told to,
To stay here and wait and wait and wait,
Waiting for news of friends also waiting
In places they didn't get to choose.

One day the waiting will be over,
We'll ask ourselves what we were waiting for,
A trick question, with no right answer,

We'll count up the days that we wasted,
The number will be very small, maybe zero,
Every day as new as tomorrow, as full as today.

6 April 2020

THE LONG GOODBYE

So many goodbyes. A photo on the New York Times website
A restaurant trying to stay open somewhere, masked waiters
Serving dinners in surgical gloves—will we ever eat out again?
Will we want to? Will we care? That was another life, wasn't it?

So many goodbyes. Film festivals, premiers, full theaters
Something to celebrate and new friends to celebrate with
Family reunions now a mortal threat, cross country trips
That used to end with a hug, countries too scary to visit

Counting goodbyes, hoping for hellos, something new
To feel good about, unsure what, or when, or why
Learning to wait without waiting for anything special

Remembering another life, sure, but not too well
A daily disappearing act—how it was. Do we really want
To go back there? Do we really have that choice?

COUNTDOWN TO YESTERDAY

Countdown to yesterday?—don't know which direction we're going,
Only that things aren't going well. We'll get there—where? tomorrow?
But will we even recognize it? In Trump's Washington, heavy nostalgia
For a time when dark skinned folk knew their place, and kept quiet.

Yesterday gets more attractive every day, not just to right-wing crazies
But liberals who thought we were getting our act together,
That innocent dumb dream of a perfectible society—the other guys
Were perhaps more realistic, went full speed ahead, backward.

They're still pretending to be good guys, mouthing good slogans.
But they'd welcome slavery if they could only figure out how
And maybe they will. The dream of equality is on life support.

Yesterday, we were all in charge, fat cats and rednecks, doing well....
Fuck those egg-heads, we had our pickups, our power boats
Our weekends at the lake. Why stop? Why did it ever stop?

DIANE

Why me? Why not someone else? Why them? Why?
Why Diane? That fierce small person, explorer
Of wild places, rivers and canyons, collector
And connoisseur of the best margaritas....

We don't know why, we never will, why try
To understand the crazy ins and outs of this life
The on-again, off-again, beauty and delight
And the headaches and sadness, never far off

Why anyone? We don't know, won't ever know
Better stop asking. Life can't wait for answers
That aren't there, probably won't ever be there

Today was a helluva day, more than good enough
Tomorrow is another flip of the coin, another surprise
I'd like good news but a beautiful sunrise will do

WAITING

Waiting to stop waiting, to know what's coming, what's already here
For real, not just a guess, a hunch, a halfhearted hope or two
Waiting takes time and time is all we have but never enough
So we wait, waiting for what we thought we wanted to happen

Finally, to get here, to say: this is it, what we've been waiting for
And then, maybe, someday, to ask if it was worth the wait
Sure, it was, but no, maybe it wasn't, and besides we're not there
Not yet, maybe never will be, don't really want to stop waiting

I guess we're waiting for tomorrow and tomorrow never arrives
It turns into today, fooled you again, there is no tomorrow
We're trapped in a permanent present, wishing for something else

Waiting for something else, always waiting, then suddenly time's up
It's over, this very moment, what we have always been waiting for
Important to chose well, a future *now* we can accept, even love

ART

If it's art is it good? if it's good is it art?
The answer, of course, is no, but why is that?
Questions loaded with other questions,
What is art? what is good? and what is 'it'?

Start with the easy part, art, well not so easy,
A challenging marriage of beauty and meaning.
Beauty without meaning is just decoration
Meaning without beauty, just philosophy

And who cares? Caring is part of the story.
Some beauty isn't beautiful at first, gotta care
Care enough to look twice, maybe once more

Let it soak in, then ask why, why so beautiful?
That's where meaning raises its hand, Why?
That's the real question, maybe art is the answer

THE BEFORE TIMES

Today Edgar was talking about the Before Times.
Everyone has their own memories, don't they?
But what was he remembering? It wasn't just easy
Although it was—no questions about the future,

Almost boring, so many yesterdays lined up
To become tomorrows, no worries, next week
Just like last week, already ready to forget.
That was the Before Time, we didn't even know it.

What does it take? a plague, a pandemic
A hurricane in the Gulf, a surprise diagnosis
A death in the family? And the door slams shut.

Can't go back there, can we? Don't want to
If we're honest. The one-way arrow of time
Is always there, always pushing us on

MAKE BELIEVE

Let's pretend, let's pretend everything is okay,
Even if it isn't, let's pretend the country is okay,
Pretend the president and his government care
What happens to other people, to you and me.

We know they don't, but let's pretend we'll all be okay,
Pretend the virus will disappear, the economy boom,
The country will be safe, school kids and grandparents too,
Pretend the elections will be free and fair, troublefree.

We can do this. We have a lot of practice pretending.
Why let reality stand in the way? Why ask for more?
More transparency, more truth, even just a little more?

Obviously we don't need it, we're too used to this,
Living in a make-believe country, telling ourselves
Make-believe stories, living our make-believe lives.

HISTORY HAUNTS US

History haunts us, painful, brutal, scarcely survived,
Then ghost written by apologists for the winners,
Almost a lie, not quite, but never totally true either,
Feel-good stories to make the heinous heroic.

Do we really need a new history? history inside out?
The schoolbook version not forgotten, just retold,
A new story—what happened, and why, and how,
How we got here, and who we hurt to get here.

Why even think about history? Will it help us?
It doesn't tell us what to do, only what not to do.
But its outline, its reflection is tomorrow's roadmap.

We're trying to wake up from history like a bad dream,
And it isn't easy. But every nightmare has bright spots,
Can we blow those embers, those moments, back to life?

2020, YEAR OF THE PANDEMIC

A challenging season—no one would have chosen this.
No one did. But here we are, all of us, every last one,
Everyone's life turned upside down by an invisible virus,
There's a lesson here I am afraid we aren't going to learn.

Not smart enough, not trying hard enough, too illiterate
Even to read the handwriting on the wall, a new chapter
Of an old story. But each new chapter raises the stakes,
Harder and harder to shrug off those terrifying tomorrows.

Remember when 'going viral' was a sign of success?
Everything is different now, and nothing is different.
Everything's up for grabs, and they're grabbing everything,

Under coronavirus cover redistributing wealth, upwards,
Shredding the safety net, burning the amazon, betting
On a market that, today, rewards only blind faith and greed.

6 July 2020

THE LITTLE SUMMER OF SAN JUAN

The hills are white, the sky grey, by noon roads are muddy,
Whatever happened to the *veranito de San Juan*?
The little summer of San Juan, winter's traditional pause?
"Tiene ganas de nevar," it wants to snow, is all they say.

And so it does. In Patagonia everyone's patient, winter's winter
No one is surprised. Last winter it didn't snow, didn't even rain
For months on end, and now it never stops, but who cares?
Daylight is stretching out, a few minutes earlier, a few later.

We're not in a hurry, we're here for the duration, for the long haul.
But we have no idea how long that is, our crystal ball is fogged,
We hunt for fresh greens in midwinter, and buy more good wine.

In the morning there's ice on every puddle, frost on the grass,
And each sunny day seems a blessing, no matter how cold.
It is. And even the bleakest, grey, overcast day is still a gift.

WATCHING FRIENDS GROW OLD

Watching friends grow old, you shake your head
How did it happen? You weren't paying attention
You're surprised without really being surprised
It had to turn out like this, you knew it all along

Although you didn't actually see it coming
A different person, a different life. Edgar said it:
"These people don't know who we used to be"
Why should they? We didn't either, did we?

The years have stolen more than muscle mass
What's left except for old habits, worn in
Worn down, worn out, by too much repetition?

Comes a moment, some stop pushing back,
They're not going anywhere, maybe they're
Already there? At least as far as they need to go

MAYBE TOMORROW

In Texas they always ask: if you're so smart why aren't you rich?
And they are seriouis about it. What we need to ask is:
If you're so smart why haven't you made a difference yet?
Why is the world still the way it is? Why can't you change it?

An embarrassing, frustrating question. With no good answer
I'm still thinking about it, you tell yourself, I'm working on it
Are you really? Is it just too hard to turn this giant ship around?
Are you helping? Am I? Is anyone? And why not everyone?

There's no good answer but a lot of bad ones, lots of excuses
We are running out of options, we're going to have to try
And it won't be easy, nothing good is, it won't be fun either

And we can't just stop what we're doing, and head off pell-mell
Toward that brave new world we want, and can't quite define
But maybe we can start, somehow, maybe tomorrow, maybe...

WINTER AT CASA MÁRMOL

Just out of reach, up there, below the clouds,
White fingers of fresh snow filling the gullies,
Reaching down toward the lake, still snowing,
Our first Patagonian winter, after all these years—

Still a lot to learn, will the water pipes freeze?
Do we have enough wood in the *leñera*?
How cold is it going to be in another month?
How much is 14 degrees Centigrade in Fahrenheit?

Winter so far is a quiet adventure, no complaints,
A new battery, ice on the windshield, car still starts,
The low sun paints our peaks with new shadows.

So far so good, doesn't feel like exile, exile from what?
Where were we going anyway? I think we must be there.
This is exactly where I belong, right here, with you.

WHERE ARE WE NOW?

Is this the end of optimism?
Is this the beginning of collapse?
Is this all we can do now?
Is this the end of an idea?

It's something else entirely
A peeling away of false facades
It's a coming to grips with....
With everything we didn't do

And pretended wasn't true
The dead end of me-first
Us-first, fat cats forever

And to Hell with them
Black or brown, or just poor
Don't say we cared, we didn't

THE EDGE OF HISTORY

Woke up this morning on the far edge of history,
On the southern sidelines, watching antarctic clouds
Scud by overhead, far from protests and police murders,
From pandemics and politicians scared of CEO donors.

Back home—we used to call it home, didn't we?—
A slow-motion judicial coup d'état is gathering steam,
The president ignores a few more rules, thumbs his nose
At a constitution he can't read, his toadies cheer him on,

Here we watch transfixed, as the internet filters our anxiety,
We ask ourselves how it happened and fall back on cliches:
"Power corrupts, and absolute power corrupts absolutely"

We try to console ourselves that our wannabe strongman
Doesn't yet have the absolute power he wants—not yet,
We pretend it can't get worse, and we worry that it will.

RAINING AGAIN

Rain on the tin roof, we can hear it drumming its thousand fingers
On the metal, but we shouldn't, it ought to be snowing now
It's winter, a mountain winter, and mountains mean snow,
At least they should. Mountains are naked without snow

They need snow the way we need sunshine, to be themselves
Higher up, the glaciers are piling up snow for summer
But we'd like to see a little more snow down here
True, we're only a few hundred meters above sea level

But Patagonia is supposedly synonymous with wild peaks
Snow plastered, wind blasted, weathered in, weathered out
Snow-covered ranges ring us on all sides, shouldn't complain

We can forgive the rain, pastures will be green again in spring,
Lambs will grow fat for Christmas *asados*, food for fiestas
We can't help ourselves, missing the sun, hoping for a whiter winter

ALWAYS THE SAME POEM

The same poem with different words
Different line breaks, different images
All interchangeable, always the same
Same theme, same ideas, same poem

I really do want to say something
Words to wake up, wake myself up
Wake everyone up, it won't happen
No one is listening, no one cares

Why should they? why pay attention
To the same question: Why? Why now?
Endlessly repeated, never answered

The poem doesn't promise an answer
Tells us there is no answer, & we believe it
For fourteen short lines, then forget

SAY GOODNIGHT

Say goodnight to another day, don't ask
If it was a good day or bad, it was both,
It always is. Maybe tomorrow will give us
Another chance....to try again, why not?

Say goodbye to tomorrow, no second chance
To get it right, to start over, to do it better
We've already placed our bets, *les jeux sont faits*
Life isn't a casino, but it might as well be

Say hello to a brand new world, one we made
Without meaning to, by accident, although
Nothing is really an accident, more like luck

Say thanks for the good luck, ignore the bad
All we can do, and precious little time to do it
Another day already disappearing behind us

HEAT MAPS IN THE NEW YORK TIMES

Maps tell the story, a certain story, bright red for hottest spots
Then orange, finally tan, and maybe, far away, cool paper white
That's one story: no water in the West, four-corners country
Dry as dust, here in Chile the opposite, reservoirs finally filled

This year at least, and no lessons learned, here or there.
We know what to do, or what we should have done already
And worse, what we are not going to do, no matter what
But we don't know why, why we can't do better

The internet is aglow with wildfires, photos and videos.
Dreams, savings, lives, everything, going up in smoke
Not just smoke, but flames, wild, leaping, red flames

Every year it's the same, or maybe every year worse
Hard to tell the difference, we shake our heads
And wonder how we got here, but really, we know.

PATAGONIA: TIMES TWO

1

Coirón—the wild wind-blown hair of the steppe
Neneo—prickly pillows of yellow-green thorns
Alamos—leftover vital signs of a lost gaucho culture
Calafate—tart purple berries waiting for a sweet return

Homesteads and fields that nobody will inherit
Vast empty spaces patrolled by the wind
Memories of *asados*, family fiestas, drunken fights
The sheep are gone now, the guanacos still here

Everything changes, Patagonia not so much
Pumas still feast on unlucky newborn *chulengos*
Condors still soar without a single wing beat

Patagonia is a ballad improvised by a *payador*
Sung then forgotten, but never written down
Full of surprises and strange haunting rhymes

2

Coirón—cabello desordenado de la estepa revuelto por el viento
Neneo—almohada flotando en el pastizal, cojín de espinas
Álamos—últimos signos vitales de una cultura perdida
Calafate—frutas agrias esperando un retorno dulce

Campos y fundos que nadie vaya a heredar
Vastedades patrulladas por el viento
Recuerdos de asados, fiestas, puñaladas borrachas
Las ovejas se fueron, los guanacos se quedaron

Todo cambia, o casi todo, pero la Patagonia no tanto
Los pumas devoran la cría inocente de los guanacos
Los cóndores siguen planeando sin mover las alas

La Patagonia es un tema improvisado por un payador
Cantado y olvidado de pronto, pero nunca escrito
Lleno de historias insólitas y rimas raras

BAD WRITING

Is sincerity enough? Depends.
Sincerity about what? Health?
Beauty? Justice? Literature?
Doesn't matter, sincerity's a start.

OK, a helluva start, especially
With sincerity in such short supply.
But if you put your heart into it
And it still isn't good, then what?

A good sentence expressing
A bad idea becomes bad
Its artfulness unforgivable.

The reverse doesn't work either
Good ideas, the best thoughts,
Lose their punch poorly expressed.

LATEST NEWS

Something else to worry about
I know it won't help, never does
the list is endless but everything ends
soon enough anyway, way too soon

Time to fix a few things, only a few
Bind up a few wounds, look away
Forget 2030, 2050, maybe next year
will be good enough, still not easy

Every day something else goes wrong
When do we get a day of good news?
Isn't that an oxymoron? news is news

If it bleeds it leads, trouble sells
Floods, fires, what's bad is good
worst is best, the very worst is Trump

PASSÉ DECOMPOSÉ

The past is fading
Where did it go?
Un petit muscadet
Dans un vieux bistro

The past is past
Time to let it go
Tomorrow's almost here
Time to say hello

Dehors il pleut
Sauve qui peut
Memories fading fast

The time's already past
How much is left?
How long will it last?

READY OR NOT

Ready to write, write what?
Ready to read, read what?
Never really ready, are we?
Never ready for the answer

The answer to a question
We weren't ready to ask
In words we only learned
To speak, but not to think

Ready to learn we don't know
What's around the corner
Of another year, another month

Ready for another surprise
Ready or not, the future is ready
To swallow us whole, & spit us out

TRUMPERTANTRUMS

When a spoiled brat
Playing President
Has a Trumpertantrum
And stamps his foot

Bangs his little fists,
All Washington trembles
Reporters report on it
Commentators comment

Usually, and thankfully
nothing much happens
He tweets and tweets

And while no one watches
Bad men do bad things
It has to stop. Will it?

UNDER COVER OF TRUMP

Under cover of Trump
They are busy stealing
As much as they can
As fast as they can

An old capitalist trick
Break up a good firm
And sell off the pieces
For an obscene profit

Republicans learned how
To do it to our country
They're doing it now

Selling off your land
Destroying your future
Under cover of Trump

WHITECAPS

The lake this evening is full of whitecaps
Hundreds, actually thousands, whipped up
By the restless, relentless northeast wind
The blue-gray water looks colder than ever

It is, but somehow we are warmer than ever
Here inside Marble House on top of this cliff
300 feet above the crashing breaking waves
The stove's been burning all day, never stopped

Why stop? Nothing stops, does it? Just pauses
Takes a breath and rushes on, we can't catch up
Maybe we are already there, here, where else?

The wind shrieks and roars, too loud to ignore
Dissonant music, soundtrack of the South
Sweeping the sky clean for another day

Oct 12, 2020 Casa Mármol

FULL MOON

Tonight's the full moon, for once it floated up over the ridges
In just the right spot, right where an artist would have put it,
Rising through a still pale sky, a moon balloon, blown up, let go.
Tonight's sky is a puzzle, is it darkening? or turning slowly pink?

Or both? It's neither this nor that, but everything, all at once
All together, last light, first dark, subtle colors clinging to the sky,
And the sky tonight, so calm, friendly, no wind, no soaring birds,
Where have they gone? It doesn't really matter, they'll be back.

What makes summer summer? Evenings that go on forever.
9:30 and it's still light, soon we'll be still waiting for sunset at 10:30
Each extra minute, each hour, each day of light is a precious gift,

Payoff for a patient winter. Patience is Patagonia's secret weapon:
Quién se apura, pierde el tiempo. In a hurry you'll only lose time.
Is that true? True everywhere? Or maybe only here in Patagonia?.

WORDS TO WASTE

Words to waste, or not, hopefully not, they should count
For something, toward something, sometimes they do
Often they don't, and whose fault is that? those who talk
Or those who listen? they're only words after all, not actions

When people say: "actions speak louder than words"
They have simply run out of metaphors, forgotten that
Words are actions too, do things, change things, silence too
Not saying something can echo just as long, just as loud

Means and ends, means to what end? What questions
Need answering? Ultimately everything we say is a question
And depending on how we say it, contains its own answer

Are there really any unanswered questions? only answers
We don't want to hear, refuse to hear, to take seriously
Answers to questions that we don't want to hear either

AFTER THE ELECTION

The aftermath isn't going that well
But we knew it would be like this
Trump lost and the world cheered
But his followers can't let go

Captains are supposed to go down
With their ships, not sink the ship
Before jumping into a gold lifeboat
And sailing off to play golf and tweet

This is all new, only it really isn't
Countries have been built and ruled
And destroyed by madmen forever

We just weren't ready, never are
So yes, for us it's a new challenge
A new chance for a brand new life

CON PACIENCIA

Con paciencia se gana el cielo, with patience you get to heaven.
Do we really want to go there? I don't think so, what about you?
But patience surely is worth something, maybe worth a lot. Why?
Because nothing, nothing good, ever works the first time around

So maybe the goal is to fail without frustration, without blame, ready
To learn what happened, and why.... Fail fearlessly, and fail again,
And finally figure it out. That's the tricky part, it's never easy
To say you were wrong, so much easier when it's someone else's fault.

But easy isn't the answer. I don't have an answer, no one does.
Being all right with being all wrong is a liberation, or would be
If only.... If only I didn't always have to be right, do I really?

No need. Dozens of failures every day, and it doesn't matter.
Dozens of successes too—somewhere everything is in balance
If only we could see it. Why not? Just accept it, just be patient.

BONSOIR DEMAIN

Bonsoir demain, où tu t'es caché?
Au revoir hier, on t'oubliera bien vite
Nous attendons un futur imaginaire,
Qui en tout cas n'est pas prêt à arriver

Bonsoir a ce passé qui nous poursuit
On pensait t'avoir laissé il y a longtemps
Le poids de tant d'années nous retient
Comment se libérer d'une vie entière?

Mieux vaudrait ne pas se disputer
Avec des souvenirs déjà douteux
Mieux vaudrait imaginer une nouvelle vie

Basée sur des plans jamais réalisés
Ni commencés, ni abandonnés
Pourquoi ne pas repartir à zéro?

19 Novembre 2020

THE LAST TRUMP RALLY?

Beatific smiles and QAnon T-shirts
Dull gaze of a true believer, believing
As hard as he can, as hard as she can
And no, it really isn't hard at all

Trump's troops, a kamikaze band
Lemmings in lockstep, over the cliff
They don't seem to care, even notice
That the game is up, their time is up

But everyone remembers their phone
Selfies are real among fake everything else
To show they were there, to show they cared

It's all they'll have when the curtain falls
When their hero runs away and hides
To count his ever shrinking ill-gotten gains

28 Nov 2020

MINIMALISM

How many words do I really need?
To say what I think I want to say
The poem not finished till every
Unneeded word is crossed out

The question is still unanswered:
What do I really want to say? & why?
At least it's good practice, good luck
Trying to figure that out, keep trying

Minimalism is a great temptation
Does it make sense? does it work?
Does it make better poems?

Maybe better, but never best....
Throw out unneeded ideas, not words
Old ideas too comfortable to change

28 Nov 2020

ANOTHER SEASON

Summer is ready, ready for what, to do what?
Spring meanwhile doesn't know which way to turn,
Hesitates, just long enough for winter to slip back in,
Then swears allegiance to summer once more.

These zig-zag seasons, coming and going, then
Coming back, then going away, again and again,
"All four seasons in one day" is what the locals say
But even so, all the fruit trees are in blossom now.

The world hasn't stopped turning, spinning, whirling
Past us, we try not to jump on board, or overboard,
We wonder if it's too late to start over, we know it is.

The seasons break and shift aound us, then shift back.
In the village the old folks say it used to be different
And young ones stare at their phones and daydream.

30 Nov 2020

CRAZY SPRING DAYS

The weather's turned inside out
Maybe upside down, a puzzle
With no answer no solution
Yesterday too hot, today too cold

Weather or not, here we are
Nowhere else, nowhen else
It's only weather not climate
And not half again as scary

There is one constant—wind
Warm days, warm winds
But usually not, clammy & cold

Our hands in our pockets
On morning walks, waiting
For summer—it's almost here

30 Nov 2020

FOUR CORNERED

The four corners of our world, why only four?
The four noble truths of Buddhism, why four?
Four seasons, at least the way we count them
Even the Navajos have four sacred mountains

Not enough or too many or maybe just right
We'll never know, don't try to puzzle this out
And what about living a foursquare life?
Or building a foursquare house? just words?

Or something else? What does anything mean?
Simply that we can count to four, although
We have ten fingers on two hands, five each

Why not just say: some. Or a lot. Or enough
Enough is always the right number, it's enough
But then we ask: enough for what? It never ends

MISTY MORNING

Sitting in my favorite chair
Looking out at my favorite landscape
My favorite person asleep in the next room
My favorite milk coffee warm in my hands

Watching low misty clouds hard at work
Dissolving the peaks, gentle steady rain
Renewing the grass, already so dry
Washing away the world's dust

Raindrops dance across the windowpanes
Two hooded hawks join my morning watch
Their feathers shedding the rain, waiting

For today to start, to see what comes
No hurry to tackle their endless task
Ferrying food to their nest, to their chicks

GROWING UP IN PATAGONIA

Growing up in Patagonia, two young hooded falcons
Caracara caranchos, just fledged, fly from tree to tree
Learning the world, how to tear a dead rabbit apart
With claws and beak, with patience, that's all they need

It's a tough world out there, a bird-eat-bird world
everything, every creature eats every other, no one's safe
No one cares, should we? Do we? We're meaner than most
Out there most aren't mean, meanness is a human trick

Growing up in Patagonia— one could do worse, right?
Clean water, clean air, no crowds, no cars, no smog
Not even enough money to tempt one toward folly

These beautiful birds didn't chose their nest
But we did, and we worry, not about a bigger raptor
But about what's next, around the corner of the year

ELECTION AFTERMATH

What are we watching now, from 6,000 miles away?
Is this the beginning of the end of democracy
An imperfect idea at best, as practiced back home
In the US, the United States of somewhere

West of Europe, East of Asia, way north of here
When—or if—the dust settles what will be left?
Democracy down for the count, & no one counting
Is this the still birth of a still unfinished project?

Democracy in a dumpster? who can you trust?
And why would you trust them? Don't bother
Money talks, and race. Class too, not so classy

I really used to believe that everything was OK
Till I lived with segregation in the 60s in Texas
But that was only Texas, now poison is everywhere

19 Dec 2020

WHY, WHY NOT?

Instead of asking Why? try Why Not?
Instead of asking When? try: whenever....
Instead of looking, searching, say: whatever....
Instead of coming home, keep on moving

What's the hurry? the calendar is blank
Days stretch out, the equinox closer & closer
And then the world turns on a dime, & shrinks
& measuring life by light, it starts to die

Not us—we say—we're in it for the duration
But we have no idea how long that might be
Yesterday was pretty good, today's better

& tomorrow better yet, until it all stops
Every day's a dress rehearsal for tomorrow
For one particular, inevitable tomorrow

CROSSING THE LINE, TRUMP REFLECTS

What now? now that we have stepped across
The blurry line between reality and reality TV
The uncertain frontier between fantasy and fact
Under cover of chaos let's make something new

How about a new definition for fact checking?
Just check your facts at the door, not needed
Any longer, we're traveling light now, unconstrained
By truth or consequences, by law or custom

It's not lying if you are not trying to fool anyone
Only yourself, and it feels so good, doesn't it?
Good manners are for losers, who needs them

Now that we have shrugged off the straightjacket
Of accountability we can finally be free—anyway
Making money is more fun than making sense

13 Dec 2020

MAKING PLANS

Making plans, as if it were still possible to make plans
As if it ever was … booking flights to a remembered world
We won't recognize if we get there, that won't recognize us
The best laid plans now suspect, but we make them anyway

Making decisions as if we had time to do everything
But no time to stop doing anything, where did it all go?
Those elastic days and years, stretching out of sight
Now they are really out of sight, out of reach too

Making a calendar of remaining time, better get busy
Making haste when we really should try to slow down
Making one more attempt to get it right, but more urgently

"All those plans that never did come true"—just a jazz song—
So many did, some were the wrong plans, many just right
Time to think about good times, maybe stop making plans?

17 Dec 2020

ENDGAME 2020

When does it stop? No answer
Nobody knows. Do we care?
Too busy being busy, normal life
Trying to stage a comeback

The year almost over, a hard act
To follow, not really worth repeating
Between politics and pandemic
We failed, illusions in tatters

We failed to save the planet
Or ourselves, from ourselves
But we never tried very hard

Tomorrow we'll get it together
Today there is still tomorrow
But It won't always be there

ZUT ALORS!

Zut alors! ¡Chuta! What the hell! I don't have the words
To say what needs to be said, even worse, I don't have
Anyone listening to hear, much less understand, what
I need to say. *What the hell!* Try to say it anyway....

I want to say: it's time for a change, a big change,
No more trying to finesse the future, to make it work.
Time to say: *No more! ¡Basta! Assez, c'est fini!*
We no longer have the time for subtle solutions.

Who is brave enough to say: nothing is working,
We have overplayed our hand, pushed it too far.
Brave enough to live as if life itself was at stake

And it is. Too many reasons, excuses, to do nothing
Greta was brave enough, there aren't enough Gretas
Wake up, the future is falling through the cracks

TELLTALE PHOTOS

Photos keep showing up, breadcrumbs
From days, lives, we have almost forgotten,
Mostly black and white, barely in focus.
Who is this person, seated at a typewriter?

What was he thinking? doing? writing?
Could this be me, or some other me?
Who is this beautiful girl seated in a cafe
In colonial cobblestone San Miguel?

Could she be the same beautiful woman
I wake up with and hug every morning?
The same person I am still in love with?

We're almost the same, still growing into
Our real selves, leaving other selves behind,
To become who we really wanted to be.

TODAY IS FOREVER

Today is forever, and tomorrow is never
Today is where we live, and tomorrow it's over
Tomorrow's too far away, we can't get there
Tomorrow is a novel we are trying to write

Or maybe read, at least to follow the story
The plot's far fetched, doesn't make sense
Agatha Christie would have done better
Hercule Poirot could have explained it

And who really cares? Today's what we've got
We can't trade it in now, can't start all over
It's what it is, what it isn't, and never will be

Tomorrow is terminal, and the future pure fiction
Still, we keep on making plans, pretending
That today isn't tomorrow's dark shadow.

CAN'T COMPLAIN

Can't complain, could, but I won't
Where would I rather be? doing what?
And with whom? This evening, here,
In the south, is all I need and more

Nobody needs this much beauty, but
Maybe that's what everyone needs
And seldom gets, not just seldom,
Almost never if we're honest, so no—

I can't complain for myself, but I will for you
For your kids, your family, your neighbors
For everyone who got a raw deal, so many

I've lost count, no one is counting, no one
Wants to know, Patagonia is not the answer
There will never be enough evenings like this

8 Jan 2021

BOOKS BY LITO TEJADA-FLORES

Backcountry Skiing

A Sierra Club guiide

Breakthrough on Skis

And its sequel:

Breakthrough on the New Skis

Say goodbye to the intermediate blues

Soft Skiing

Effortless low-impact skiing for older skiers

This is Skiing

The impossible romance of sliding over snow

with photos by Linde Waidhofer

Wildwater

A Sierra Club guiide

Parables and Fictions

Short stories & narrative experiments

For No Good Reason

Cimbs & climbing, mountains & mountaineering

Still Crazy in Love

Poems for Linde Waidhofer

Maybe a Sonnet

Lito's first book of sonnets

Mi Idioma Prestado

Poems in Spanish

& multiple photo books from Western Eye Press

in collaboration with Linde Waidhofer

Lito Tejada-Flores is addicted to short,
mostly unrhymed 14-line poems,
sonnets of a sort. Born at 13,000 feet
in the Bolivian Andes, he's spent most
of his life in the mountains, or thinking
about mountains, climbing them, skiing
them, admiring them, and sharing them
with as many people as he can, as a ski
teacher, filmmaker, writer, publisher, book
designer, and occasionally, poet. He lives
half the year in Chilean Patagonia, half the
year in the Colorado Rockies, with his true
love, photographer, LInde Waidhofer.

You can write Lito at

litotf@westerneye.com

www.ingramcontent.com/pod-product-compliance
Lightning Source LLC
Chambersburg PA
CBHW051800040426

42446CB00007B/449